Arthur Rackham

Edited by David Larkin
Introduction by Leo John De Freitas

A Peacock Press/Bantam Book
Toronto * New York * London

With special thanks to Mrs. Barbara Edwards,
daughter of the artist.

An original PEACOCK PRESS/BANTAM BOOK

We are most grateful to the publishers, libraries, museums and private
collectors who have kindly allowed the use of material in their copyright.

ARTHUR RACKHAM

Library of Congress Catalog Card Number 75–11188

PRINTING HISTORY:

First U.S. Edition: August, 1975

Bantam Books are published by Bantam Books, Inc. Its trademark, consisting
of the words "Bantam Books" and the portrayal of a bantam, is registered in
the United States Patent Office and in other countries. Marca Registrada.
Bantam Books, Inc., 666 Fifth Avenue, New York, New York 10019, U.S.A.

Published simultaneously in the United States and Canada

PRINTED IN ITALY BY MONDADORI, VERONA

One and all, we at some time fabricate a 'world of our own;' a world in which we are both creator and participant. Infants play happily with 'friends' unseen and unknown to anyone but themselves. Older children are able to weave highly descriptive tales, and delight in the intricacies of costume, character and plot. However, in only a few of us is the creative intimacy of these fabulous worlds kept alive, and nurtured, through the years that lead to adulthood.

To a select few is given the gift of recalling, revisiting and, thankfully, reproducing their worlds of fantasy. And within this elite company Arthur Rackham must be considered as one of the select among the select. To him was given the energy, skill and extravagant vision which combined to make real the realm of imagination; which combined to produce an ever-lasting vision of Faery.

But what is one likely to encounter in Rackham's land? Who might one be rubbing

shoulders with? Where will faery paths lead us?

If such a suggestion of chronology is valid in the world of faery, the period that predominates in Rackham's imagination is that in Northern Europe when the land was covered in vast forests and when scattered farms and hamlets, mercantile towns and the occasional wealthy city were brief, but always welcome respites to any traveler. Not infrequently the tamed and sophisticated countryside of his beloved Southern England makes an appearance in the illustrations, but the enchantments of deeply shadowed forests always draw him back.

Occasionally too, there is a response to the Classical traditions in English literature in some Arcadian and idyllic scenes, but not for long does he linger there. The opulence and easy living of Arcadia never seduce him away from the harsh and exacting life of the northern forests. One is not likely to find smooth-skinned, roseate and plump people often in Rackham's work. Quite simply, they could never have survived beneath the almost perpetual autumnal skies, and the constant reminders that life is a harsh taskmaster.

It is not known whether Rackham

intended his illustrations to carry, in any way, moral undertones, but in his work it is possible to detect suggestions of asceticism – a life of austerity. But then, perhaps the dominating atmosphere is one of fatalism and the stoic endurance of a begrudgingly benevolent Nature. There are undoubtedly other interpretations – the land of Faery is a puzzle if nothing else.

Rackham's fertile imagination gave him access to such disparate worlds as thirteenth-century Germany, the France of Louis XIV and Victorian England, but practically always there are suggestions of the fascination he felt for forests and trees, and all the mythology that goes with them.

But who might one expect to meet while journeying with the artist? Certainly the denizens of the woods – and in the strict sense of the word can we ascribe to his weird creations the status of citizenship. The mythical characters are truly an integral part of the forest community. The various sprites and elves are *really* derivative of the bark and branches of the trees in which they live, and of the earth upon which they tread. The gnarled and exposed roots of massive beeches are to be found in the long, knotted fingers of woodland imps. The ochreous hue of bole and earth is reflected in the unhuman coloring of elves. Faces fuse with cracked and twisted bark; eyes and mouths distort into holes and knots of aged trunks.

After a while one can begin to question whether faces are really staring out of the illustrations, or whether one's own imagination has recognized, independently of the artist's intentions and guidance, the essential features of yet another face. And of course this is the bonus of having Arthur Rackham's work in front of you. Besides fulfilling their role as graphic interpretations of an author's text, the illustrations are often separate entertainments full of the delight of discovery. Without hindering their explanatory function Rackham frequently enriched his drawings with cleverly disguised faces and figures, and the reader is invited to amuse himself in their detection.

Besides harboring the mythological peoples of the forests, the trees themselves are often personified. One illustration, not included in this collection, depicts an 'arboreal family' at their toilet. An elderly relative remonstrates with an unruly sapling struggling to escape from its

mother's attention. The mother patiently persists in passing a comb through the tangled mass of twigs or hair. Certainly a 'fantastic' domestic scene, but one which sums up Rackham's sensitivity to the trees life cycle. From sapling to fallen and decaying corpse he depicts joy and agony, pride and vanity. Surely he believed these emotions must be felt by such magnificent examples of life, and by drawing them for us with, at first glance, improbable personalities he gently guides us toward sharing his beliefs.

Into this land trespass the humans. Bare-footed woodlanders, less disadvantaged perhaps than their city cousins, but none the less for that still outsiders, beautiful princesses, gallant young knights, farmers, merchants, the foolhardy and the bewitched. They are as much ill at ease, and at risk, here in the forest as they are confident and secure in their palaces and farms. The finery and delicacy, so much a *sine qua non* of the sitting-room and ball-room, is mocked by the harshness of the woods. The daintily slippered foot and the slightest of rose blushes, so admired by suitors, encumber pretty maidens lost or forsaken in the forest depths.

It is these contrasts, between the human and the mythological, the sophisticated and the rude, the gentle and the austere, that enthrall us. Rackham has been called The Beloved Enchanter, and spellbound we can become. Frightened, beguiled and somehow alone, we identify with the isolated human in a world once thought familiar, now horribly alien.

But where else might we venture? And who else might we meet? Away from the forests (but never from the persistent textures of wood) we are likely to stumble upon an ogre's castle or a giant's den. From the gaiety and warmth of the tavern or palace we might awake to the chill of a dragon's lair or the quaintness of a dwarf's cottage. Across the gentle swell of tilled downlands we might tramp until wearied, and rest on a bleak and barren moor, mystified as to how we got there.

Rackham acknowledged a remote influence from Japanese art (the linear quality of Japanese prints in particular was admired by the majority of late Victorian and Edwardian decorative artists), and one might expect to trace such an influence in the examples of dragons and other mythological beasts he drew. However, this is not the case. Certainly his dragons have all the essential characteristics of their species: serpentine body, scaly skin, wings, talons and the ability to breathe fire; but the heavily stylized Chinese or Japanese dragon is very far removed from the generally ponderous and evil-looking creations of Rackham.

Take, for example, the dragon in the illustration 'How Sir Lancelot fought with a fiendly dragon' (plate 21). The knight has just released the dragon from a tomb, and its bulky proportions suggest the cramped lair that had conditioned its growth. One might consider that this dragon is diminutive, as far as dragons go, and not particularly worthy of such a legendary knight as Lancelot du Lac. But the thick scaly neck and leathery body attest its strength, and the sulphurous smoke and barbed flames the ferocity of its onslaught.

At the opposite end of the size scale, and more suggestive of Far Eastern art work, we have the three-headed Chimera battling Bellerophon and Pegasus (plate 35). A combination of lion, serpent and goat, this fabulous monster rears and rallies from the valorous warrior's attack. An incredible creature certainly, but one which appears to have offered no problems to Rackham's

agile mind. The difficulty of combining the three such disparate animals has been resolved in a simple, but masterly way.

From the dragons let us consider for a moment the giants and the ogres. Although often lean and knobbly, the giants convey brutish power and mentality. If they can string cattle and pigs from their belts and throw them across their shoulders, what on earth could they do to us! Whether crashing through farmyards like the giant Cormoran (plate 27), or 'sniffing out' Englishmen like the ogre in 'Jack and the beanstalk' (plate 25), we are never at ease until some hero comes along to put them in their place.

But what can we say of the heroes and heroines? Whether expensively arrayed princes and princesses, or barefoot farm lads and country lasses, they all share common qualities. Sensible and resolute, they look robust and noble no matter what the origins of their birth. They are all 'comely and sound of limb.' They are ideal young men and women, but then in the world of faery we are generally dealing with extremes: intelligence and stupidity, wisdom and foolishness, beauty and ugliness.

And then there are the bewitched, and

those in peril of enchantment. Suddenly made deaf and dumb by the 'little people,' the princess stands frozen in shock as the curse holds her (plate 17). Guleech, the hero, clenches his fists and makes as if to attack the leader of the faery host, but the grotesque little man leaps into the air on his broomstick, angrily gloating at the boy.

Although lamentably distressed, the beautiful princess is not so tragically affected as those hapless souls from Milton's *Comus* (plate 31). At one time ordinary people, these pathetic creatures have supped of the treacherous sorcerer's 'orient liquor', and having lost their human faces are transformed into the hideous creatures we see here. Completely ignorant of the metamorphosis, they bedeck themselves with the plumage of a kingfisher and a dove and 'boast themselves more comely than before.' The brutish woman with hairy arms, feline eyes and heavily boned face is truly an ugly and repulsive creature, and yet how convincingly Rackham has drawn her conceit.

But not all the fair maidens are susceptible to the spells of the fairy-folk. Some are strong enough to resist. Look how valiantly Lizzie refuses the exotic but enchanted fruit of the goblins from Christina Rossetti's *Goblin Market* (plate 39). Pressed against the tree, pulled at, stamped on and clawed, she refuses to part her lips lest the terrible goblins force her to eat. Even the tree appears to mock the poor girl, but her resolution holds.

The realms of faery and myth were not the only fantastic and macabre worlds Rackham knew. His illustrations to Edgar Allen Poe's *Tales of Mystery* show the illustrator's skill in the more intense and nightmarish world which borders that of the balanced and sane.

The illustration from *The Pit and the Pendulum* (plate 40) depicts the tortured man on the brink of the pit as the red-hot walls close in on him. In seconds he will be burnt to death or thrown to a slow and horrible end unless a miracle happens. The contorted shapes on the walls appear to suggest graphically the losing of the senses, the distorted vision of a man about to faint.

These somewhat desperate and depressing moments are captured in other stories and books, and Rackham is not at pains to continually sentimentalize or beautify his audience's world. The illustration 'Young Bekie' (plate 29) from *Some British Ballads* elicits surprise and

revulsion from us before we can begin to sympathize with the young swain's condition. Prior to escape, Bekie lies ragged and wretched on the filthy dungeon floor. The artist spares us nothing of the prisoner's privations, and the luckless lad's experience of being overrun with foul rats knawing at his hair and clothes seems an unnecessary choice of subject. Certainly there are more wholesome passages in the story from which a different subject could have been chosen, but the reversal of the young man's fortunes (with an ultimately happy ending) is originally approached from this illustration of his early humiliation and plight.

Rackham's illustrative work, as already seen, is not only interpretative of texts but fun to look at in its own right. Often there are visual clues in a drawing that the unwary will miss. For example, the statuette of the Venus di Milo in the bedroom of the cat transformed by that goddess into a beautiful woman (plate 10). The positioning of the candlesticks and the figurine, and the arrangement of the mantelpiece generally, suggest a devotional corner, or altar, to the patron deity. Again, the distressed gentleman in the illustration 'As I was going to St Ives' (plate 14) must surely be a self-portrait of the artist in middle age.

Like so many of the artists and illustrators working at the turn of the century Arthur Rackham took full advantage of the developments in new printing processes. When he was born, in 1867, wood engraving was the predominant method by which an illustrator's work was reproduced. However, when he made his debut in book illustration in the last decade of the century, the new photomechanical line block process had become a major threat to the older process. The illustrations in this collection show how Rackham fully appreciated, and skilfully used, the three-color printing process which flourished from the opening years of the twentieth century.

At his death in 1939 Arthur Rackham was internationally known and respected. Throughout his career he had had many imitators, and indeed today a number of modern illustrators are unable to ignore the particular fascination he had felt for the atmosphere and texture of forests and trees. Needless to say, their work does not equate with his. The best of them acknowledge his vision and influence and pass on, hopefully to develop their own unique styles; the rest

perish in the brilliance of his work. It is hoped that this beautifully reproduced collection will help enhance the reputation Rackham already enjoys among genuine lovers of good book illustration, and will excite those who might be sampling his magic for the first time.

Leo John De Freitas
May 1975

1) They all crowded round it panting
and asking, "But who has won?"

Alice's Adventures in Wonderland
By Lewis Carroll

WILLIAM HEINEMANN LTD.
1907

2) The Pool of Tears

Alice's Adventures in Wonderland
By Lewis Carroll

WILLIAM HEINEMANN LTD.

1907

3) "An unusually large saucepan
flew by it, and very nearly
carried it off."

Alice's Adventures in Wonderland
By Lewis Carroll

WILLIAM HEINEMANN LTD.

1907

4) Come, now a roundel.

A Midsummer Night's Dream

WILLIAM HEINEMANN LTD.

1908

5) The Infancy of Undine
Undine
By De la Motte Fougue
WILLIAM HEINEMANN LTD.
1909

6) Undine outside the window

Undine

By De la Motte Fougue

WILLIAM HEINEMANN LTD.

1909

7) The Rhine's pure-gleaming
children told me of their sorrow.

The Rhinegold and the Valkyrie

WILLIAM HEINEMANN LTD.

1910

8) Wotan. "Appear, flickering fire,
encircle the rock with thy flame.
Loge! Loge! Appear!"

The Rhinegold and the Valkyrie

WILLIAM HEINEMANN LTD.

1910

9) The Lion, Jupiter,
and the Elephant

Aesop's Fables

WILLIAM HEINEMANN LTD.

1912

10) Venus and the Cat

Aesop's Fables

WILLIAM HEINEMANN LTD.

1912

11) The Two Pots

Aesop's Fables

WILLIAM HEINEMANN LTD.

1912

12) The Shipwrecked Man
and the Sea

Aesop's Fables

WILLIAM HEINEMANN LTD.
1912

13) There was an old woman
lived under the hill

Mother Goose
The Old Nursery Rhymes

WILLIAM HEINEMANN LTD.

1913

14) As I was going to St. Ives

Mother Goose
The Old Nursery Rhymes

WILLIAM HEINEMANN LTD.
1913

15) Old Mother Goose

Mother Goose
The Old Nursery Rhymes

WILLIAM HEINEMANN LTD.
1913

16) Hey! Diddle Diddle!

Mother Goose
The Old Nursery Rhymes

WILLIAM HEINEMANN LTD.

1913

17) "Now, Guleech, what good
will she be to you when she'll
be dumb? It's time for us to
go – but you'll remember us,
Guleech!"

The Allies' Fairy Book

WILLIAM HEINEMANN LTD.

1916

Now reprinted by Heinemann in 1974 as
FAIRY TALES FROM MANY LANDS

18) At the dead time of the night
in came the Welsh giant.

The Allies' Fairy Book

WILLIAM HEINEMANN LTD.

1916

Now reprinted by Heinemann in 1974 as
FAIRY TALES FROM MANY LANDS

19) Art thou warm, Maiden?
Art thou warm, Pretty One?
Art thou warm, my Darling?

The Allies' Fairy Book

WILLIAM HEINEMANN LTD.

1916

Now reprinted by Heinemann in 1974 as
FAIRY TALES FROM MANY LANDS

20) How Arthur drew his sword Excalibur
for the first time.

The Romance of King Arthur
Abridged from Malory's
Morte D'Arthur

MACMILLAN & CO.
1917

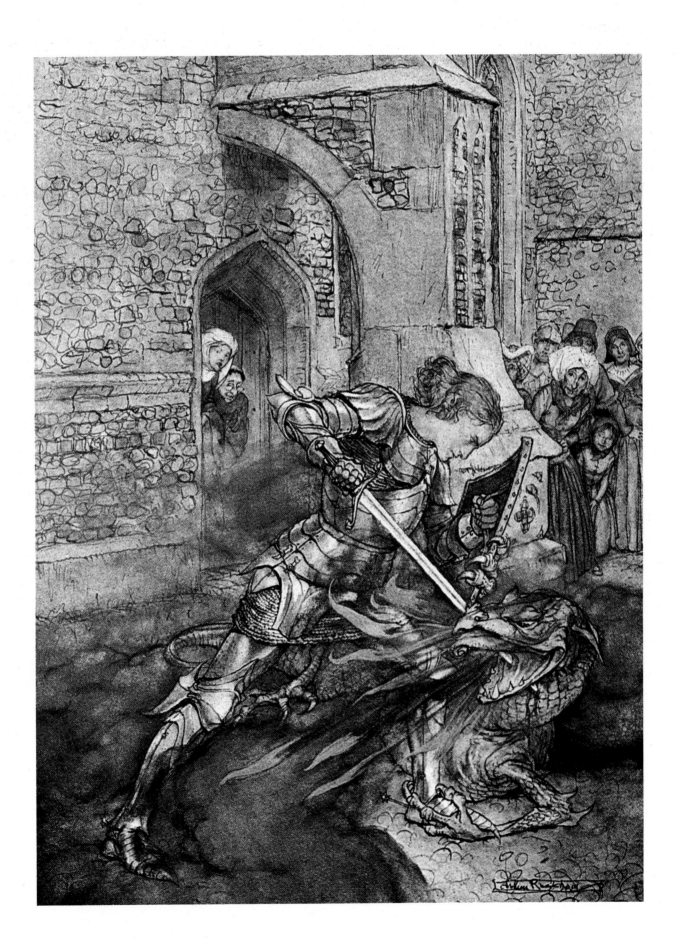

21) How Sir Lancelot fought
with a fiendly dragon.

The Romance of King Arthur
Abridged from Malory's
Morte D'Arthur

MACMILLAN & CO.

1917

22) What did she find there but
real ripe strawberries.
Little Brother and Little Sister
and Other Tales by the Brothers Grimm

CONSTABLE & CO.
1917

23) They thanked Her and said
good-bye, and she went on her
journey.

English Fairy Tales
Retold by F. A. Steel

MACMILLAN & CO.
1918

24) She went along, and
went along, and went along.

English Fairy Tales
Retold by F. A. Steel

MACMILLAN & CO.
1918

25) "Fee-fi-fo-fum, I smell the
blood of an Englishman."

English Fairy Tales
Retold by F. A. Steel

MACMILLAN & CO.
1918

26) Taking the keys of the castle,
Jack unlocked all the doors.

English Fairy Tales
Retold by F. A. Steel

MACMILLAN & CO.
1918

27) The giant Cormoran was the
terror of all the country-side.

English Fairy Tales
Retold by F. A. Steel

MACMILLAN & CO.
1918

28) Mary Colven

Some British Ballads

CONSTABLE & CO.

1919

WILLIAM HEINEMANN LTD.

later 1919

29) Young Bekie

Some British Ballads

CONSTABLE & CO.
1919
WILLIAM HEINEMANN LTD.
later 1919

30) Clerk Colville

Some British Ballads

CONSTABLE & CO.

1919

WILLIAM HEINEMANN LTD.

later 1919

31) And they, so perfect in their misery,
not once perceive their foul disfigurement,
but boast themselves more comely than before.

Comus

WILLIAM HEINEMANN LTD.

1921

32) It seemed as if a sudden
swarm of winged creatures
brushed past her.

A Wonder Book
By Nathaniel Hawthorne

HODDER & STOUGHTON
1922

33) There was no danger, nor trouble
of any kind and no clothes to be
mended, and there was always plenty
to eat and drink.

A Wonder Book

By Nathaniel Hawthorne

HODDER & STOUGHTON

1922

34) Pandora and Epimetheus

A Wonder Book
By Nathaniel Hawthorne

HODDER & STOUGHTON
1922

35) Its three heads spluttering
fire at Pegasus and his rider.

A Wonder Book
By Nathaniel Hawthorne

HODDER & STOUGHTON
1922

36) Sometimes he suspected that he loved them as God does – at a judicious distance.

Where the Blue Begins
By Christopher Morley

WILLIAM HEINEMANN LTD.

1925

37) . . . and sometime voices

The Tempest

WILLIAM HEINEMANN LTD.

1926

38) When night was come and the
shop shut up.

Fairy Tales by Hans Andersen

GEORGE G. HARRAP & CO.

1932